STEM Careers

BOTANIST

Helen Lepp Friesen

MEDIA ENHANCED BOOKS
AV2 BY WEIGL
ADDED VALUE • AUDIO VISUAL

www.av2books.com

AV^2 provides enriched content that supplements and complements this book. Weigl's AV^2 books strive to create inspired learning and engage young minds in a total learning experience.

Go to www.av2books.com, and enter this book's unique code.

BOOK CODE

AVR52523

AV^2 by Weigl brings you media enhanced books that support active learning.

Your AV^2 Media Enhanced books come alive with...

Audio
Listen to sections of the book read aloud.

Video
Watch informative video clips.

Embedded Weblinks
Gain additional information for research.

Try This!
Complete activities and hands-on experiments.

Key Words
Study vocabulary, and complete a matching word activity.

Quizzes
Test your knowledge.

Slide Show
View images and captions, and prepare a presentation.

... and much, much more!

Published by AV^2 by Weigl
350 5th Avenue, 59th Floor
New York, NY 10118
Website: www.av2books.com

Library of Congress Control Number: 2019938822

ISBN 978-1-7911-0918-9 (hardcover)
ISBN 978-1-7911-0919-6 (softcover)
ISBN 978-1-7911-0920-2 (multi-user eBook)

Printed in Guangzhou, China
1 2 3 4 5 6 7 8 9 0 23 22 21 20 19

052019
103118

Project Coordinators: Heather Kissock and John Willis
Designer: Ana María Vidal

Every reasonable effort has been made to trace ownership and to obtain permission to reprint copyright material. The publishers would be pleased to have any errors or omissions brought to their attention so that they may be corrected in subsequent printings.

Weigl acknowledges Alamy, Getty Images, iStock, Shutterstock, and Wikimedia as its primary image suppliers for this title.

STEM Careers

BOTANIST

Contents

What Is a Botanist?

Botanists are scientists that study plants. This science is called botany. Botanists learn about the parts of plants. They understand how plants eat and grow. Botanists are always looking for new kinds of plants. If they find plants they have never seen, they try to identify them. Some botanists focus on plant **conservation**. Other botanists study how plants are **classified**.

There are many different kinds of botanists. Marine botanists study plants in water. Agronomists study plants that grow on farms. Plant taxonomists identify different kinds of plants.

The work botanists do is important. People depend on plants for healthy living. Botanists research how the **environment** affects a plant's health. Botanists can help discover new cures for diseases. They do research on how plants cure illnesses. Botanists can also find new ways of using plants for food.

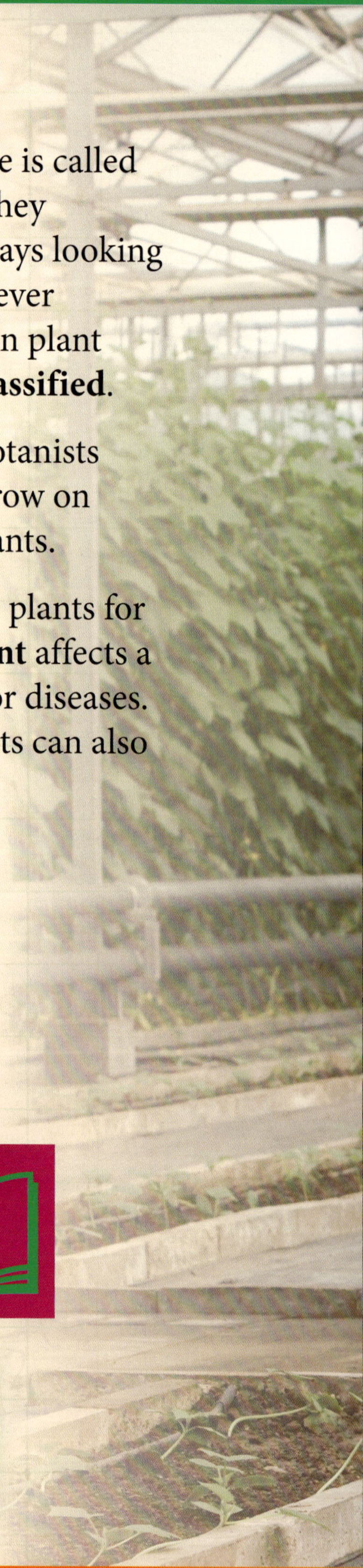

There are close to **400,000** different kinds of plants.

The American Society of Plant Taxonomists has more than **1,100** members. The Society publishes two yearly **botany** journals.

The Conservatory at the **United States Botanic Garden** in Washington, D.C., houses 12 permanent and 2 seasonal gardens.

Botanists who work in botanical gardens study new plant species and new ways to use plants.

A STEM Job

Botanists work in the field of STEM. STEM stands for Science, Technology, Engineering, and Mathematics, or math. STEM is a developing field. Jobs in STEM change as new tools and techniques are created.

Botany is a kind of science. Botanists with science jobs do **experiments** and ask questions. This helps them understand what helps plants grow. Technology has changed how botanists do their jobs. Today's botanists use new tools to learn about plants. They study plant **cells** using powerful **microscopes**.

Future of STEM Jobs

By 2022, most STEM jobs will be in technology. Some future STEM jobs may not even exist yet.

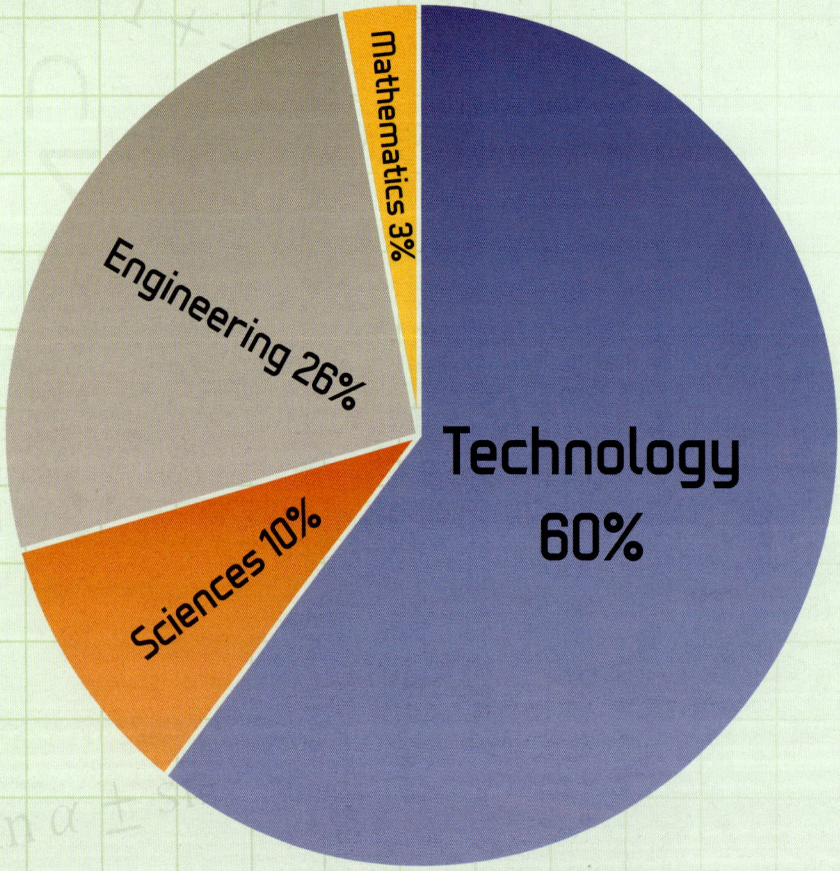

Engineers solve problems and build things, including greenhouses. Some botanists change plants or make new plants. This is called **genetic** engineering. Botanists who work in math explore numbers and patterns relating to plants and how they grow. They use math and science to see how plants react to weather and pollution.

Through lab experiments with seeds, botanists have learned to change the way farmers grow certain crops.

Swedish botanist **Carl Linnaeus** came up with **groups** for all living things in the mid-1700s. They are still used today.

The **Linnaean** system assigns two names to every species.

There were **six classes** of animals in Linnaeus's first system, including mammals, fish, and insects.

Linnaeus originally divided plants into **24 classes**, or groups.

Arboretums and Botanical Gardens

Botanists work in places where there are plants. Plants may be outdoors or inside buildings. One day, botanists may be looking at plants under a microscope. The next day, they may be collecting plants outside. The work of botanists can take them into rainforests or deserts.

Arboretums and Botanical Gardens in the United States

There are botanical gardens and arboretums in all 50 states. Many have special themes. Some feature plants from one area, while others have plants from around the world.

Desert Botanical Garden
Phoenix, Arizona

Some botanists work in greenhouses and **laboratories**. Others work in schools and colleges. They teach and do research. Botanists can work on farms. Some work for the government. They give advice about issues that affect plants, such as pollution. Many botanists work for **arboretums** or botanical gardens. They create new **exhibits**. Visitors ask them questions about plants.

Botanists often meet with other scientists. They share their research at meetings and conferences. Botanists might give speeches at museums or colleges. Many botanists write about their work for magazines.

United States Botanic Garden
Washington, D.C.

Kanapaha Botanical Garden
Gainesville, Florida

A crop scientist is a botanist who studies ways to help farmers grow crops in all kind of conditions.

All in a Day's Work

Air, soil, and water are all important parts of a botanist's job. They study plant habitats. This helps them learn what helps or harms plants. They study how dirty air changes plants. They might also research the best way to clean up oil spills around plants. Botanists also work with conservation programs. They find ways to protect and save **endangered** plants. They work to protect plants from **erosion** and pollution.

Botanists study the different parts of plants. The plants they study can be huge trees or tiny **organisms**. They study the small parts of a plant to learn about how plants work. Botanists may also find different ways to grow crops. They may help farmers grow more vegetables, or fruits that need less water to grow. Botanists teach people about protecting the environment.

Sample Daily Schedule

Botanists are constantly learning new things about plants. They read about new discoveries. They try new lab technology. Many botanists collect plant samples and study them in their labs.

8:00 AM

A botanist collects soil and plant samples in the woods. She will study the nutrients, or vitamins and minerals, in each sample. The botanist is collecting research for a report she is writing. She wants to know how soil affects plant growth.

11:00 AM

The botanist takes the soil and plants to her lab. She will look at them under the microscope. Each plant was grown in a different type of soil.

12:00 PM

The botanist gets the lab equipment ready for her research. She sets up the microscope. She makes sure all the parts are clean and working. The botanist studies the plants and soil under the microscope. She begins making notes for her report.

2:00 PM

The botanist meets with coworkers at the botanical garden. They are getting ready for a visit from a local school group. The students are studying rare plants.

3:00 PM

She returns to the lab to finish her research. The botanist reviews the plants and soil samples. She continues to make notes about them for her report.

4:00 PM

The botanist cleans up the laboratory. She puts away equipment. Work stations need to be left clean for the next day.

Using the Scientific Method

Scientists use the scientific method to solve problems. The scientific method is a series of steps. It begins with a question scientists want to answer. First, they find out if another scientist has asked the same question. If so, they review the scientist's results and gather information for their work. Next, they make a hypothesis, or guess about the answer to the question. Then, scientists test the hypothesis with an experiment. After the experiment, they form a conclusion. This means they study the results and decide if the question was answered. Finally, scientists share the results with the public and other scientists.

1. Ask a Question

Does light affect how plants grow?

2. Construct a Hypothesis

Plants need light to grow. Plants will grow better in a well-lit area.

3. Test with an Experiment

To test the hypothesis, grow six bean plants. The plants should all have the same soil, pot, and room temperature. Place half of the plants in a well-lit area. Put a dark cloth over the other half. Measure the height of the plants every day for two weeks. Measure how many new leaves there are on each plant. Write down the numbers each day.

4. Did the Test Work?

To answer the question, look at the daily measurements. Compare the growth of the plants in the light and in the dark.

5. Draw Conclusions

Based on the test results, plants need plants need light to grow. The bean plants in the well-lit conditions grew much better than the ones that were under the cloth. Therefore, the conclusion is that plants need light to grow.

Tools of the Trade

Botanists use many tools in their work. They use different items for different jobs. Laboratory work requires special tools. Working with plants outside requires other tools. Botanists carry some tools with them. Other tools are kept in offices and labs.

Pruning Shears

Pruning shears are clippers. They are used for cutting plants. Their blades are very sharp. Botanists need them to make careful cuts to plants. They do not want to damage plants without reason.

Trowel

A trowel is a small, sharp hand shovel. It is used to remove plants from dirt, soil, or sand. A botanist only takes what he or she needs when digging up plants. A trowel helps the botanist remove a plant without harming other plants. Botanists also use trowels when planting seeds and working with plants in greenhouses.

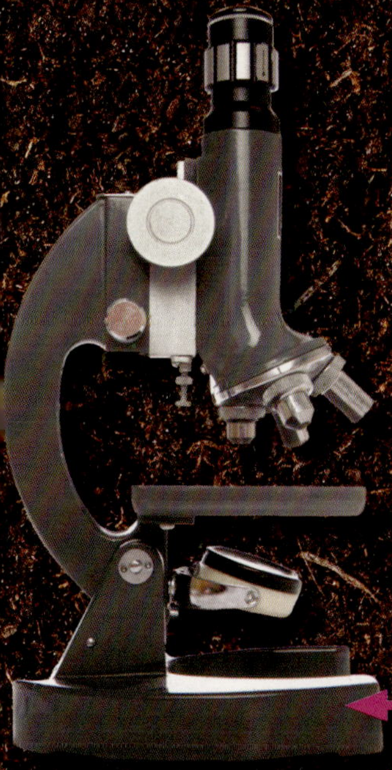

Microscope

A microscope is used for looking at the smallest parts of plants. Botanists use staining when they study plants under a microscope. They put a special liquid called dye on the plant. The dye turns parts of the plant different colors. Staining makes very small parts of the plant, such as the cell walls and the nucleus, show up clearly under the microscope.

Camera

A camera is used to photograph plants. Some plants cannot be removed from nature. Botanists use cameras to take pictures of them. Photos allow botanists to compare and identify plants and plant parts. Many microscopes come with built-in cameras. Botanists can take pictures of a plant's smallest parts.

Then and Now

The word botany comes from the ancient Greek word *botan*. This means "pasture" or "plants." People have studied plants for thousands of years. The tools used by botanists have changed a great deal over time.

Then

The first microscopes were curved pieces of glass. They were more like big magnifying glasses. Early microscopes made small things look up to 10 times bigger. Zacharias Janssen and his father Hans were eyeglass makers. In the 16th century, they put one piece of glass on each end of a tube. This made small objects look even bigger. Scientists such as Galileo used their idea to make better, stronger microscopes.

Now

Today's microscopes are very strong. They can make objects look 1,000 times larger. Microscopes are used to see things that the human eye cannot see. Some microscopes help scientists see things as small as **atoms**. Scientists can connect microscopes to computers. This lets them share what they are seeing with others.

The Botanist's Role

The work of many botanists involves **climate change**. Earth's climate is always changing. Climate change affects people and animals. It also has an effect on plants. If the temperature is too hot or too cold, plants have fewer days to grow. This could cause them to die or stop producing seeds. Then, the plants might become endangered. People's actions can harm plants, too. Factories and cars create pollution, or dirty air. Polluted air makes it hard for plants to grow. Chemicals people use for cleaning can drain into the soil. This can cause plants to die. Botanists help people make better choices about their actions.

Studying plant growth in a lab helps botanists understand how seeds react to different weather conditions.

Botanists also use biotechnology. Biotechnology means changing the way a plant grows. Botanists expose plants to different weather conditions. They expose plants to harmful chemicals. Then, they use genetic engineering to change the plant's cells. Botanists develop plants that grow in any kind of weather. They grow plants that are not harmed by pollution or chemicals. Farmers are able to grow crops even when there is a drought. Astronauts can grow fresh vegetables in space. The work of botanists makes this possible.

Astrobotany

The National Aeronautics and Space Administration (NASA) is using astrobotany, or the study of plant life in space, to give astronauts fresh food. Astronauts on the ***International Space Station (ISS)*** grow seeds in a special plant habitat. The plants provide fresh vegetables for the astronauts. They also clean the air inside the space station.

It costs about **$10,000** to send one pound (0.45 kg) of food supplies to the *ISS*.

A. thaliana was the first plant grown in space, in 1982.

NASA's **Advanced Plant Habitat** has more than 180 sensors and 3 cameras to monitor plant growth.

Becoming a Botanist

People who want to become botanists are good at asking questions. They enjoy doing experiments. Students interested in botany pay attention to details. They are curious and patient. Would-be botanists love nature. They like looking at plants in the forest. Those interested in botany enjoy growing plants from seeds. Young people who are interested in botany might like collecting leaves or helping with the family garden.

Students who want to learn about botany take biology and chemistry in high school. Biology teaches them about different kinds of plants. They study how they grow and where they live. In chemistry classes, students learn about the **elements** that make up living things. Would-be botanists learn to be organized in high school. They learn to take notes and write essays. These skills prepare them to be successful in college.

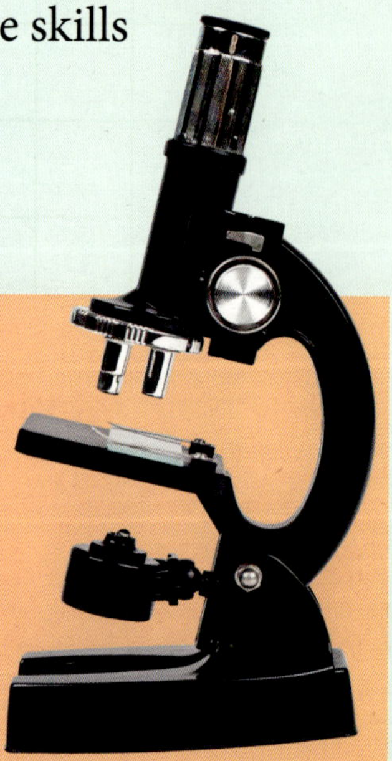

Botanist Salaries

Salaries for botanists are based on where they are employed. Some botanists make up to about $143,000 per year

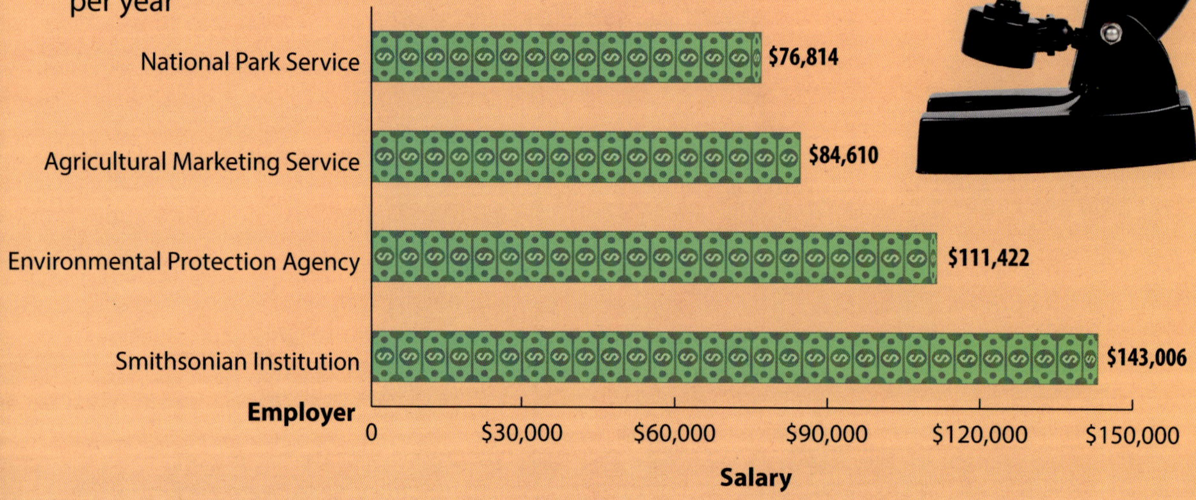

Botanists must keep careful lists of the plants they identify and study each day.

Is This Career For You?

Botany is a good career choice for people who love nature. However, not all botany jobs are the same. You might spend all day in a lab. You might travel to faraway places for research. You might even teach a class about plants. A career in botany may be a good idea if you are willing to do all of these things.

✓ Training

Training to become a botanist starts in college. You will take many science classes. Some will teach you about parts of plants and different kinds of plants. You will also take classes about endangered plants and plant conservation.

✓ Education

Get a bachelor's degree in botany. This takes four years of college study. Some botanists get higher degrees in botany. These degrees can help you get top-level jobs. Earning these degrees takes up to four more years of college.

✓ Application

Attend job fairs to learn more about places where botanists work. Look for job openings on the internet. Contact botanical gardens and science centers that hire botanists.

Career Connections

Plan your botanist career with this activity. Follow the instructions in the steps below to complete the process of becoming a botanist.

A Talk to people who work in the field. Ask about the work they do. Read blogs written by botanists. Learn about the many different kinds of jobs in the field.

B Find out where you can study botany. Visit a job fair or a college career center. Learn more about the work of a botanist.

C Work on your future resume. A well-written resume shows a potential employer that you have the skills for the job.

D Look for local gardening clubs online. Meet others who are also interested in plants. Find out if you can volunteer at a local garden.

1. Decide if you have the personality to become a botanist. If you enjoy doing research and experiments with plants, this job may be for you.

2. Consider the different places botanists work. Think about which ones you like best. Many botanists work in gardens. Others work outdoors in fields and forests.

3. Research what different botanist jobs require. Contact employers and learn what they look for in applicants. Look for ways to develop the skills you need.

4. Apply for a specific position. Arrange for an interview. If they contact you, go to the interview. Be prepared with a strong resume and good skills for the job.

Quiz

1. What is botany?
2. What does STEM stand for?
3. Why might a botanist take a picture of a plant?
4. What basic education is required to be a botanist?
5. Where are some of the places botanists work?

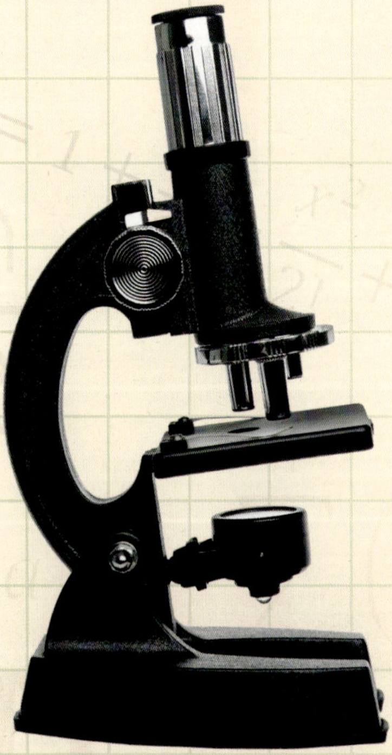

6. What is the purpose of pruning shears?
7. How much does it cost to send fresh food into space?
8. What is the purpose of staining?
9. How many different kinds of plants are there?
10. A botanist who works for the National Park Service makes about how much money per year?

Answers

1. The study of plants
2. Science, Technology, Engineering, and Mathematics
3. Because it cannot be removed from its environment
4. A bachelor's degree in botany or plant science
5. Laboratories, colleges, nature centers, and botanical gardens
6. For cutting plants
7. About $10,000 per pound
8. To show parts of a plant that are hard to see
9. Close to 400,000
10. $76,814

Key Words

arboretums: botanical gardens devoted to trees

atoms: the basic units of all things

cells: the smallest parts of any living thing

classified: organized or arranged

climate change: weather patterns that change over a long period of time

conservation: the preservation of Earth's resources

elements: substances made from one type of atom

endangered: at risk of going extinct

environment: everything living and nonliving on Earth

erosion: the natural process of moving soil and rocks from one place to another

exhibits: items or collections on display in a museum

experiments: tests used to discover or prove something

genetic: related to the features that pass naturally from one living thing to another

***International Space Station (ISS)*:** a large satellite in space where astronauts live and study for long periods of time

laboratories: rooms designed for scientific experiments

microscopes: instruments for viewing small objects

organisms: living things made of one or more cells

Index

Log on to www.av2books.com

AV² by Weigl brings you media enhanced books that support active learning. Go to www.av2books.com, and enter the special code found on page 2 of this book. You will gain access to enriched and enhanced content that supplements and complements this book. Content includes video, audio, weblinks, quizzes, a slideshow, and activities.

AV² Online Navigation

Audio
Listen to sections of the book read aloud.

Book Pages
AV² pages directly correspond to pages in the book.

Video
Watch informative video clips.

Embedded Weblinks
Gain additional information for research.

Key Words
Study vocabulary, and complete a matching word activity.

Try This!
Complete activities and hands-on experiments.

Quizzes
Test your knowledge.

Slideshow
View images and captions, and prepare a presentation.

AV² was built to bridge the gap between print and digital. We encourage you to tell us what you like and what you want to see in the future.

Sign up to be an AV² Ambassador at www.av2books.com/ambassador.

Due to the dynamic nature of the internet, some of the URLs and activities provided as part of AV² by Weigl may have changed or ceased to exist. AV² by Weigl accepts no responsibility for any such changes. All media enhanced books are regularly monitored to update addresses and sites in a timely manner. Contact AV² by Weigl at 1-866-649-3445 or av2books@weigl.com with any questions, comments, or feedback.